The House that Jack Built

A Diverting Story

Illustrations by Rodney McRae

A Young Yearling Special

This is the

house that Jack Built.

This is the malt

that lay in the house that Jack built.

This is the Cat,
that Killed the Rat,
that ate the malt,
that lay in the house that Jack built.

This is the Dog
that worried
the Cat
that killed
the Rat

that ate
the malt

that lay
in the
house
that Jack
built

This is the Cow
with the crumpled horn,
that tossed the Dog,
that worried the Cat,
that killed the Rat,
that ate the malt,
that lay in the house that Jack built.

This is the Maiden all forlorn,
that milked the Cow
with the crumpled horn,
that tossed the Dog,
that worried the Cat,
that killed the Rat,
that ate the malt,
that lay in the house
that Jack built.

This the Man
all tattered and torn,
that kissed the Maiden all forlorn,
that milked the Cow with the Crumpled horn
that tossed the Dog,
that worried the Cat,
that killed the Rat,
that ate the malt that lay in the house
that Jack built.

This is the
Priest
all shaven and shorn
that married the Man all tattered and torn,
that kissed the Maiden all forlorn,
that milked the Cow with the crumpled horn,
that tossed the Dog,
that worried the Cat,
that killed the Rat,
that ate the malt,
that lay in the house that Jack built.

This is the Cock
that crowed in the Morn,

that waked the Priest all shaven and shorn,
that married the Man all tattered and torn,
that kissed the Maiden all forlorn,
that milked the Cow with the crumpled horn,
that tossed the Dog,
that worried the Cat,
that killed the Rat,
that ate the malt,

That lay in the house
that Jack built.

This is the Fox

that lived under the thorn

that stole the Cock

that crowed in the morn

that waked the Priest all shaven and shorn,
that married the Man all tattered and torn,
that kissed the Maiden all forlorn,
that milked the Cow with the crumpled horn,
that tossed the Dog,
that worried the Cat,
that killed the Rat,
that ate the malt,

that lay in the house that Jack built

This is Jack with his Hound and horn.
that caught the Fox that lived under the thorn,
that stole the Cock that crowed in the morn,
that waked the Priest all shaven and shorn,
that married the Man all tattered and torn,
that kissed the Maiden all forlorn,
that milked the Cow with the crumpled horn,
that tossed the Dog,
that worried the Cat,
that killed the Rat,
that ate the malt,
that lay in the house that Jack built

This is the Horse,

of a
beautiful
form.

that carried Jack

with his Hound and horn,
that caught the Fox that lived under the thorn,
that stole the Cock that crowed in the morn,
that waked the Priest all shaven and shorn,
that married the Man all tattered and torn,
that kissed the Maiden all forlorn,
that milked the Cow with the crumpled horn,
that tossed the Dog,
that worried the Cat,
that killed the Rat,
that ate the malt,
that lay in the house that Jack built.

This is the Stable
so snug and warm,
that was made for the horse
of a beautiful form,
that carried Jack with his Hound and horn,
that caught the Fox that lived under the thorn,
that stole the Cock that crowed in the morn,
that waked the Priest all shaven and shorn,
that married the Man all tattered and torn,
that kissed the Maiden all forlorn,
that milked the Cow with the crumpled horn,
that tossed the Dog,
that worried the Cat,
that killed the Rat,
that ate the malt,
that lay in the house

that Jack built.

This is the Boy
that every morn
swept the stable snug and warm,

that was made for the Horse of a beautiful form,
that carried Jack with his Hound and horn,
that caught the Fox that lived under the thorn,
that stole the Cock that crowed in the morn,
that waked the Priest all shaven and shorn,
that married the Man all tattered and torn,
that kissed the Maiden all forlorn,
that milked the Cow with the crumpled horn,
that tossed the Dog,
that worried the Cat,
that killed the Rat,
that ate the malt,

that lay in the house that Jack built.

This is Sir John Barley Corn

that treated the Boy that every morn,
swept the stable snug and warm,
that was made for the Horse of a beautiful form,
that carried Jack with his Hound and horn,
that caught the Fox that lived under the thorn,
that stole the Cock that crowed in the morn,
that waked the Priest all shaven and shorn,
that married the Man all tattered and torn,
that kissed the Maiden all forlorn,
that milked the Cow with the crumpled horn,
that tossed the Dog,
that worried the Cat,
that killed the Rat,
that ate the malt,
That lay in the house that Jack built.